# What Other Marketing Books Won't Tell You

## A Brutally Honest Account of Marketing A Small Business

By Louise Palmer

I0476652

Copyright © 2015 by Louise Palmer.

All rights reserved. No part of this publication may be reproduced, distributed, or transmitted in any form or by any means, including photocopying, recording, or other electronic or mechanical methods, without the prior written permission of the publisher, except in the case of brief quotations embodied in critical reviews and certain other non-commercial uses permitted by copyright law.

# Contents

# Introduction

This book is not a 'how to make a million in your first year' book. If that's what you are looking for, you probably need to go back to your Amazon search results. Instead, this book provides a real account of marketing a small business over seven years.

In this book I will share with you the marketing I have tried to boost sales, what has worked and what hasn't.

I have read a number of business books. These books have claimed that if I follow their advice, I can make my business profits sky-rocket. I will talk you through the lessons these books preached and once I tested them, how effective they were.

I am hoping that the story of my business journey provides you with some insight, saves you from wasting time, answers some of your questions and gives you ideas for your own business.

This book is written in chronological order from the start up of my business in 2008 to 2015. Therefore you will notice certain marketing efforts show up again and again as I try different marketing ideas.

Of course every business is different. Just because one marketing idea didn't work for me, it doesn't mean it won't work for you. I think every business has to trial different marketing strategies to find what works for their business.

## My Business

To put this story into context, I had better explain what my business is. I set my business up In 2008 after I had just qualified as a Business Psychologist. I was confident I would be able to sell my consultancy services at the £825 a day that was recommended for consultants in my field. After 6 months with no work, I had to change my business. I stopped offering the consultancy work and started to offer training courses.

The business is still running today and I still love every minute that I spend working on it. Business people often refer to their business as 'their baby', and I am definitely in this camp.

# Marketing Efforts

## Template And Custom Built Websites

Once I decided to start the business, the first thing I wanted to do was set up a website. I didn't want to pay a fortune for it so decided to look at companies which offered template websites.

## Template Website

Initially I looked at some companies which offered template websites for free. The free sites would not allow me to have my own domain name. Rather than being able to have www.mycompanyname.co.uk, I would have had to have www.templatewebsite.com/mycompanyname. Although this probably would have been okay for a starting point, I wanted it to look professional. I wanted my business cards to show my company domain name.

I searched on the Internet for a template site that allowed me to use my company domain name. The template website I chose was very easy to edit. All I had to do was edit the text and the images. There were a number of templates for me to choose from. The site was quite limiting as I had to select a colour theme but could not change the colours beyond this. I wanted to change the colour of certain elements and change the layout of my website but was unable to do this.

I was really pleased with my website and it hadn't cost me much to create, only about £45. I thought it looked incredibly professional and I proudly showed it to everyone I knew. I remember the design clearly, it had a black background with white lettering and some large corporate looking photos at the top.

At the time I was lucky enough to be receiving business coaching from my local council. As part of this coaching I was able to submit various aspects of the business to a panel of experts for their review and feedback. At the very beginning of my time with them, my business coach and I sent over the information about my business and included a link to my website. One of the first things that came back was that my website was terrible. It was obviously a template site and it looked unprofessional. Apparently, it had to go.

This was quite a surprise to me. I had anticipated negative feedback about my business idea or the services I offered, but I never imagined they wouldn't like the website. Looking back on it now, I wonder if they disliked the template website because I was offering a high-end business service. Perhaps if I was running a different type of business, they would have found a template site acceptable.

## Custom Built Website

As part of the business coaching I received, I was offered funding to improve certain aspects of my business. They offered to pay for a professionally designed website for my business. I was so pleased. I met with the web designer who was one of the panel members and discussed my ideas with him. He created the website and I believe his fee would have normally been £400. The website was fairly basic. It had a number of pages with just photos and text. It also had a newsletter sign up box. I had no need for a shopping cart at this stage.

It looked great in my opinion, really professional with eye catching colours. Now that I could compare this site to my template site, I could see why they said that my template site was terrible.

I was pleased that I did not have to pay the £400 for the website at the time. I knew it was cheap compared to some websites but it was a lot of money for me to find at the start-up phase. I had just finished university and so was in quite a lot of debt at this stage.

## Google Analytics

My web developer introduced me to Google Analytics which I found was a great tool for analysing how people were behaving on my website.

I was able to see how many people were visiting my website. In the early days I would excitedly check my analytics every day. I was lucky if 2 or 3 people had stumbled across my website that day. Quite often I would check the analytics and find that nobody had visited my site. It was a bit disappointing.

I am quite a geek when it comes to statistics and enjoyed analysing the website traffic. I discovered that Google Analytics would enable me to find out various information about my visitors. I could look at what the most popular Entry Page was. The entry page was the page people tended to land on when they first visited my website. For me, it was my home page. Google Analytics also allowed me to look at my Exit Page. This was the page that people were on when they decided to leave my site. I did not have one particular page that was usually a person's exit page. If I did, I would have looked into changing this page and trying to keep people on the site for longer.

The average length of time people spent on my web site was just under two minutes. It might not sound a long time but as it was an average, I was quite pleased with this statistic.

My bounce rate hovered between 40% and 60%. I learned that the bounce rate shows the percentage of visitors who visited my site and then left before looking at any other pages. A 100% bounce rate would mean that 100% of people were landing on my website and instantly clicking off. They were not wanting to visit any other pages. A 0% bounce rate would mean that when people entered my website, they always at least visited one more page.

I wanted to see what the ideal bounce rate was for a website and discovered it should be lower than 50%. Although mine wavered around this figure, I felt pretty happy with it.

I could get completely absorbed in Google Analytics. I enjoyed looking at the acquisition section. This section told me how many people were finding my website. From this I could see if people found me via social media, a direct link (they typed my web address in their web address bar), search engine or a referral (they found my website on another website.)

If the person came to my site from a referral, it told me who the referring site was. I found this was a really useful tool as sometimes I didn't even realise that people were linking to my website.

If the person came to my site via a web search in Google, Google Analytics would tell me the search term that the person used. This was often quite interesting in itself. Often the term matched a particular sentence in my website. It seemed that people had searched for a particular psychological model and I had mentioned it on my website. On a number of occasions I would put their search term into Google to see where my website showed in the search results. Strangely, I could not see my website in the search results anywhere. I never understood this.

I also liked to look at how many visits each page had. This way I could see which were the most popular pages and therefore which service was gaining the most interest. At this point I was only trying to sell consultancy services on the website and hadn't yet made a sale.

## Free Listings On On-line Business Directories

Once I had got the new website up and had incorporated my Google Analytics, I decided to list my business in the free business directories on the Internet. These directories allowed me to create a business profile for free which included my business name, contact details, business description and a link to my website.

The sites offered the option to pay to have my advert at the top of the search results, but I decided against this as with no sales it was too much of a risk. As I hadn't actually done any consultancy work, I didn't have any reviews to include either.

The free directory listings did not bring in any business. Even to this day, they have not brought in any sales. I think the free directory listings can help certain businesses just not mine.

## Networking

After listing myself on the free business directories, I decided it was time to get networking. I felt pretty convinced that I would at least make a few sales from networking.

The first networking event I went to was an all women's event that cost £20. This was quite a strange affair. When I walked into the entrance I was met with a large chocolate fountain. The room was full of business stalls. So I deduced at this point that you could hire a stall, advertise your business and network with other people looking around the stalls. As there was no focal point, it made networking at this event very difficult. Lots of people were just milling around on their own. I decided to ignore my nerves and just start talking to someone. I spoke with about 5 people that evening and we stuck together. None of us were brave enough to move away from this temporary friendship group even though the conversation had long moved on from what our businesses could offer. We exchanged cards but I have never spoken to any of these people since.

The next event I tried was a little better organised. It was at a large manor hall and the networking event was held in a marquee. It took me ages to find this marquee in the manor hall grounds and I can remember feeling really on edge when I finally arrived at the right place. This time I walked into a room full of people. They had already formed into small groups and were chatting away. I felt pretty daunted. What was I supposed to do in this situation? Select a group, walk up and just introduce myself. This is probably exactly what I was supposed to do. Instead I went to the bar and got myself a drink. It was much easier to strike up conversation at the bar with one or two people rather than launch myself into conversation with a group of people who were already talking. I left at the earliest opportunity and felt that I had wasted another £20.

People always spout the mantra 'it's not what you know, it's who you know'. As I believed this, I persevered with the networking. I decided to try a different tack and this time went 'speed-networking'. I figured this would be much easier for me to handle. The event would be highly structured. I would be sat in front of someone and only had 90 seconds to talk about my business. The event would enable me to meet lots of different people rather than just a handful.

The event went as expected. When I arrived, we were all sat down in a designated area. The organisers told us exactly what would happen and for the first time in my networking experience, I felt comfortable. We had to sit opposite another person and speak about our business. I thought this would be fairly easy but actually it was pretty difficult. I wish I had prepared a 90 second presentation before attending the event.

At the end of the event I could have a drink and chat further with the people I'd met. I didn't feel that I had connected with anyone and therefore left again at the earliest opportunity. It just felt too awkward. I had a lot of business cards at the end of the night, but once again I have never spoken to anybody from this event since.

Persevering still, I decided to try a breakfast club. I had heard that you all sit around and eat breakfast while someone at the front talks to you about a business related matter. This sounded ideal to me.

I arrived at the event and was seated on a table of 8 people. I was so nervous I could not eat the full fry-up and opted for a single piece of toast. This was pretty embarrassing in itself as everyone on the table started asking me why I wasn't eating the proper breakfast. I started to wish I hadn't gone at all. The networking event started off with each person on the table talking briefly about their business. It suddenly dawned on me that all the people around my table were employees of large companies. This might have been great if they were senior managers or CEO's but they weren't. They were assistant level employees. They had no purchasing power whatsoever. The reason their companies had sent them was to sell to other companies but not the other way round. They could afford time out of the office for their assistants, but the people with the buying power were safely tucked behind their desks at the office.

At one of the many networking events I tried, I bumped into a lady that I had met once previously when I was working in a previous job. We struck up a conversation and found that we were both offering training services. We met up for coffee in the few weeks after the networking event and have been meeting up once every few months for about 6 years. It is great to have someone to bounce ideas off. She has given me some great ideas in the past and she says that I have done the same for her. Again, neither of us have been able to get any work from the other person, but we do make each other feel less isolated.

## On-line Business Networking

I have also tried some on-line business networking websites. There were a few social networks that were designed specifically for businesses. I found myself spending whole afternoons on one business networking site, called Ecademy, talking to like minded business owners. One person I was speaking to was interested in working with me on a joint project. We met up for a drink and discussed some ideas. In the end we created a whole new training course. It took months of work. Unfortunately, we were never able to sell this course but I have remained friends with him ever since.

Another site that I used was LinkedIn. This again is a business social networking site. Once again I did not receive any sales through LinkedIn despite spending hours and hours on the site. I still have a profile on there and these days I have over 500 connections. Still, it has not brought me in any business.

## D.I.Y. Search Engine Optimisation

About 3 months in to running the business, I realised that networking wasn't working for my business. I decided I needed to get my website on to the first page of Google. I discovered that the process of trying to get on the first page of Google was called Search Engine Optimisation or SEO for short. Each website has an SEO score which determines where it appears in the web search results.

A website's SEO score is a combination of a number of factors and Google is changing these factors all the time. After looking at all the information, I decided that I would try to improve my SEO score myself. There were companies offering to do it for me, but I still hadn't made any sales at this point and I could not afford to pay their fees.

At this point I was only offering consultancy work and wanted to be on the first page of Google when people typed in the words 'Business Psychologist, Norwich'.

Researching SEO at the time (about 2008) I found there were various things I could do to try and get my website to appear on the first page of Google.

## Registering The Website With Search Engines

Firstly, I registered my website with all of the major search engines. I typed into Google 'register my website with Google' and followed the instructions. I did the same for the other search engines.

## Keywords

Next, I needed to decide what my keywords were. I discovered that keywords were the words and phrases that I thought people would search for on web search engines to find my business. So for example, some of my keywords were 'Business Psychologist, Norwich' 'Business Consultancy, Norwich.'

I found a keyword tool by searching for 'Keyword Tool' on the web. I decided to use Google's keyword tool as it was widely recommended. The keyword tool told me how many people searched for different keywords in the last month. I could apply different filters such as whether people searched for those exact words or if the search term was just generally similar. I wanted to specify my local geographic location as I was sure that I would be able to find enough work locally. Obviously the keywords based on just Norwich had far less traffic than the nationwide searches.

I can't remember the exact figures for how many people were searching my keywords but there must have been some people or I wouldn't have pursued it.

I researched SEO keywords on the Internet and most articles suggested that I needed to optimise for about 10 different keywords. It seemed to me that I needed to decide which keyword I most wanted to optimise for and then I would also need another 9 relevant keywords.

Once I had decided on my keywords, I needed to mention them throughout the text on my website. I mentioned my keywords in my website title. The website title is the under-lined title that appears in the search results on web search engines. My website title included the keyword that I most wanted to optimise for. I also had to write a website description that would appear under the website title in the search results. My website description also included at least a few of my keywords.

From my research on the Internet, I found that the actual text on the website also counted towards the SEO score. I read that I needed to put a title on each page and if possible include my keywords in the titles. On my website I had different title options called H1, H2 and H3. According to my research, I had to use H1 for SEO purposes.

I followed the advice and mentioned my keywords in the first and last paragraphs of the text that I had written on the web page. I also included keywords here and there for the paragraphs in-between. I had some images on my website and used my keywords in the image descriptions as this would apparently also help to improve my SEO score. I paid particular attention to my home page as this was said to be the most important page for SEO. I made sure that my main keyword was mentioned on this page about 5 or 6 times.

**External Links**

My research on the Internet informed me that links from other people's websites to my website were very important for a good SEO score. These are sometimes referred to as external links or back links. When I was first doing the SEO work on my website, advertising links counted. I registered my company on lots of business directories that allowed me to put a link to my website. In 2015, advertising links no longer count towards your SEO score.

I had heard of a back link checker tool that would tell me what websites were linking to my competitor's websites. My idea was to make a list of all the websites that linked to my competitors. I could then visit each website and see if I could also put a link on their website to my website.

I searched for a back link checker tool and found quite a few results. Some of them would only let me search once a day, whereas others didn't set any limits.

The back link checker tool was really useful. I made a list of all the websites that linked to my competitors and then visited these websites. I managed to get my website listed on a number of websites that I would not otherwise have even considered.

I emailed some of the websites to ask if I could have a link from their site to mine, but never heard back. Presumably, my competitors had managed to get a link to their website due to a contact they had within that company.

**Google Maps**

I also registered my business with Google Maps. This meant that when somebody searched for 'Business Psychologist, Norwich' I would come up in the map search results. I used my business name as the title for my map result. I could have chosen a more keyword rich title and included my main keyword alongside my business name, but I felt confident that I could get on to the first page of Google without needing to do this.

**Fresh Content**

My research on SEO suggested that I needed to keep my website content fresh. I already had a blog section on the website and decided I would write a regular blog. I kept this up for about a month before I started to run out of ideas for articles.

## Changes To SEO Score

I found that working on the SEO took up a large amount of my time. I worked on it for weeks and weeks, researching how to improve my SEO score and implementing the changes. I noticed that after making the changes it would usually take a few weeks before my website appeared higher in the search results. Apparently it takes Google some time to get around to looking at websites and any changes that have been made.

## Check Progress With Google Analytics

I found it was useful to use Google Analytics to see if people were finding my website via the keyword terms I had optimised for. I wasn't getting much search traffic at the time but the occasional person would search for one of my keyword terms. Unfortunately, it was usually only 2 or 3 people a month.

## Hitting Number 1 In Google

In mid 2008, after employing the SEO techniques mentioned above, I achieved my goal. It had only taken me a few months and I was number one in the Google search results. I couldn't believe it. I was sure that this was it, I was going to make a stack load of cash. My business would start thriving and I would start earning the money I had always dreamed about. I had heard everyone saying that if your website was number one on Google, you would have a constant stream of business. So I waited. And waited. And the phone never rang. The emails never came. It had not made any difference to me at all. I couldn't understand it at the time.

## Packaging Services In To Off-The-Shelf Products

About 6 months later and still no sales, I decided to change the business from offering consultancy work to offering training courses. The consultancy work had no fixed prices and it was difficult to say how much anything would cost as there were too many factors. The training courses had a fixed price and people knew exactly how long they would last. My biggest learning point in my first year was that 'People Like Packages'. Once I had packaged my knowledge into a training course, I made my first few sales within the following weeks.

Packaging my service made a real difference. If I didn't move away from the consultancy service and package my knowledge as a training course instead, I don't think my business would have ever got off the ground.

## Door-To-Door Flyers

I mentioned in the section above, that after packaging my product into training courses, I made my first few sales. These sales came as a direct result of delivering door-to-door flyers to local businesses.

My first step was to create an eye catching flyer. I found the best way to create a flyer was to look at other flyers from businesses in the same industry. I looked specifically at flyers which were offering training courses to businesses. I was able to design a similar flyer which looked professional. Although I was a one man band, I wanted potential customers to believe I was a large company. This was only because I felt the professionals I was targeting would be put off by a one man band.

I created the design using a professional drawing programme. Fortunately, for me my father used the software everyday for his business and could show me the basics. I also managed to learn a lot of design techniques from Internet articles and You Tube. I did try to use a few free drawing programmes first, but found that they didn't quite do what I needed them to do. I found they often made objects snap to a grid, meaning that I couldn't position the objects exactly where I wanted them. The drawing programme I used was about £70. I chose to go for an older version in order to get a cheaper price. To this day I still use the same drawing programme, albeit a newer version. It has saved me hundreds, if not thousands, in graphic design fees over the years.

Once I had designed the flyer I needed to make sure the flyers looked professionally printed. I looked into printing costs at local printers and found that they were far too expensive. Even the local copy shop wasn't much better. I decided to invest in a laser printer. I previously had an ink jet printer which in my mind made everything look home-made. I figured the laser printer would give my flyers the professional look I was desperately craving. I tried a few laser printers and the first couple I tried were terrible. In the end I found a great colour laser jet printer for just over £200. It was one of the best purchases I ever made.

Printing on the laser jet printer made my business look instantly more professional. The printed colours had a lovely glossy look to them. They looked like they had been printed at the printers but they cost me a fraction of the price. I also invested in a guillotine in order to make my flyers into A5. I tried to use scissors initially but I couldn't cut a perfectly straight line.

I made sure that I used a good quality paper. I printed on 160gsm which is a thick paper and very nearly a light card. The usual paper from the supermarket is often about 80gsm. I found the best prices were online when I bought 6 or more packs of paper in one go.

I made a list of all the businesses I wanted to post flyers to in the city centre. I mapped out a route and estimated it would take about 3 hours. One night every week I would walk the streets and post the flyers through all the business doors.

When I made my first few sales this way, I was over the moon. I kept going round the same businesses every week with the flyers but no more sales came. I probably did this for about 8 weeks, if not more. Eventually I had to admit that this was not really a viable option. I needed to try something else.

## Handing Out Flyers In A Busy Area

I decided that I wanted to try handing flyers out to people in my local city. I figured that if I did it at lunchtime, lots of business people would be on their lunch breaks. I wasn't sure if I was allowed to do this so phoned my local council to check. They informed me it was fine on one condition; if people dropped a lot of flyers and the council had to clean them up, I would be charged the cleaning up fee. I hoped that people wouldn't just drop my flyers as litter and decided to take the chance. I felt a bit self-conscious handing out flyers as it wasn't something that I had done before. I dragged a friend with me to make me feel more at ease. On the day I stood in one of the busiest parts of the city and started to hand out my flyers. I targeted anyone who was well dressed and looked like they worked in an office.

It felt incredibly awkward. I offered my flyers out to people and most people either walked straight past me or said no thank you. I had envisioned that people might even stop and chat to me about my business but this didn't happen. I think after an hour both my friend and I felt deflated and were tired of feeling awkward. We called it a day. I think in an hour we managed to hand out about 20 leaflets between us. I didn't get any sales as a result.

## Web Banner

There were only so many businesses I could market to via door-to-door leaflets. I wanted to market to more businesses in my local area.

I decided to advertise with a local newspaper. I opted for a web banner which would show at the top of their website for one month. There were other companies using the web banner option, so my advert would only appear some of the time. The newspaper handled all of the design work. I just had to tell them what I wanted the advert to say. The company based the design of the advert on my website graphics to make sure the branding matched.

The web banner went live and nothing happened. I checked my Google Analytics and after one month of advertising I had only received 2 clicks, which did not result in any sales. There may be a number of reasons my advert did not receive more interest. It could have been the wording of my advert, the product or the product cost.

## D.I.Y. Search Engine Optimisation For New Keywords

Now that I was offering training courses rather than Business Psychology consultancy work, I needed to re-do my search engine optimisation work. I had previously optimised for 'Business Psychologist, Norwich' and this was no longer relevant. I needed to optimise my website for different words such as 'Conflict Resolution

Training' and 'CPD Training'. I thought that I would be able to apply the same rules and my website would appear high up on Google. I realised I might not reach number one due to the fact that I was now competing nationally rather than focusing on Norwich. Once I amended my keywords and my website page titles etc., I searched for my website in the Google search results. After reaching page 10 on Google with no sign of my website, I gave up looking any further. I decided to stop working on the SEO.

At this point I finally understood why being number one on Google for the search term 'Business Psychologist, Norwich' made no difference to my sales at all. Not many people, if any, were searching for a Business Psychologist in Norwich.

**Google Ads**

As I could not get my business to show in the Google search results, I decided to try a paid advert through Google Ads.

I set up my account and looked at the prices for the keywords I wanted to promote. I discovered that different keywords cost different amounts, depending on the competition. For most of my keywords, it would cost me a few pounds every time someone clicked on my advert on Google. When a person clicked on my advert, they would be redirected to my website. I didn't have much money to spend on marketing at the time so set my budget to £40. Once the £40 had been spent, my advert would stop.

My advert went live and I could see that people were clicking through to my website. In Google Analytics I learned that I could see the number of people coming to my website via my keywords using either the paid ad or a natural organic search.

The £40 budget was used up and I had not received a sale. As money was tight I was reluctant to spend any more money on increasing my Google Ad budget.

## Promotional Materials

As I had sold a few training courses via the door-to-door leaflets, I was preparing to deliver my first training course. I was feeling excited. I decided that I needed to purchase promotional pens and delegate folders for the training day. When they arrived in the post, I knew I had made the right decision. Although they weren't cheap, I believe they made the difference between looking professional and looking unprofessional. For the next four years I bought promotional folders and pens with my business name and logo on them.

I hoped that the delegates would keep their pens and as a result hopefully book another training course. I made sure that the pens weren't cheap in the hope that people might feel uncomfortable throwing them in the bin. I was not close enough to my clients to see if they used them at work on a daily basis. I am not sure whether or not these pens made any difference.

## Car Magnetics

I also wanted more people in my local area to know my business name. I decided to use magnetic signs on my car for my business. These were great, I could put them on the car and take them off whenever I wanted. I don't think they brought me any work but I definitely saw people looking at them.

## Entrepreneur Networking

After being put off networking for a few years I decided to try again. I had been receiving emails about an entrepreneurs networking event. The people attending this event were the business owners. This seemed like a great idea to me. I would actually meet with people who had the buying power.

I went to the event and there was a business talk. This time the business talk was about something that really interested me. It was about branding and marketing. I sat on a table with about 4 other people. I got chatting to the man next to me and he was pretty much the only person I spoke to all night. At the end of the presentation, I decided to go and speak to the presenter. It seemed we had some common ground and I met with him again in the following weeks. I am still in touch with him to this day. No work has come my way as a result. He is just another business contact that I can call on for advice if I need to. I didn't go back to this networking group simply because at the time I could not afford to. They wanted an annual membership fee of £125 plus £20 per networking session that I attended. At this stage I felt that networking was a good way to make some 'business friends' but not a great way to sell my business. My time and money could be better spent elsewhere.

My experiences of networking do not make me think that networking doesn't work. I think it can work, but I think that you have to put a lot of time in and aim to make friends with people first. I have never sold anything as a result of attending a networking event.

## Posting Flyers To Local Businesses

I wondered if I could get some sales from reaching different businesses. If I could make a few sales from putting leaflets through business letter boxes in Norwich, then surely posting flyers to businesses on the outskirts of Norwich was a sure fire way to get some more sales.

I decided to send 100 flyers to my target market. I sent the flyers to businesses within 25 miles of Norwich. Unfortunately, I didn't get any sales as a result. As postage costs were fairly high I decided not to try this again. I felt that whilst the flyers had got my business started, they weren't a viable option to keeping it going. Instead I turned my attention to email marketing.

## Unsolicited Email Marketing

Although I had a 'sign up to our newsletter' option on the website, only two people had signed up. I therefore needed to create a small database of people's email addresses to send my email marketing to. I found that if you went on to company websites, there was very often an 'About Us' or an 'Our People' page. On these pages it would list the employees and their contact information. Sometimes, this contact information included their direct email address. This was perfect for me. Emailing was essentially free and I could market directly to the people I needed to.

I wanted to check that I was allowed to send email marketing messages to the email addresses that were listed on the company websites. I was worried it might be considered SPAM which I knew was against the law. I researched it and found an organisation called the Information Commissioners Office in the UK. They provided lots of information on who I could and couldn't email. I learned that each country had different email marketing laws and these could change fairly regularly.

At this time in the UK (2008), I could email businesses. It was okay for me to send marketing emails from a business to another business (business-to-business marketing) without prior permission. This is often called unsolicited email marketing or cold email marketing.

I was not allowed to email from business to customer (business-to-consumer marketing) without prior permission. For example, I could not go on to a social media website to gather lots of people's email addresses and then email them. If I wanted to email private consumers, I would need to get their permission first. This is called 'opt-in' email marketing.

Part of the law in the UK stated that I needed to provide the person I emailed with instructions as to how to remove themselves from my list. Initially, I did not have an automatic unsubscribe link and instead asked them to reply to my email with the word 'Remove' in the subject header. I also needed to include my office address at the bottom of each email.

Once I had researched all the legalities of sending out my email marketing, I created my email. I had created a database of 500 email addresses for my first email marketing hit. I sent the email out and within a few days I had received a few orders. So I spent the next week adding more email addresses to my database. The next week I sent out another email hit, this time to 750 people. Once again, I received more orders as a result.

Email marketing was working. I realised that all I had to do was continue to build my email database. I started to spend days, evenings and weekends manually adding email addresses to my database, usually while watching TV to keep the boredom at bay. As the list of emails grew, so did my sales.

Most of my sales were to large government departments, blue chip companies and national solicitor and accountancy firms. The job level of the people booking the courses ranged from entry level roles to senior management including some Chief Executive Officers (CEOs).

In the email marketing I would put a web link to a certain page on my website. After sending an email marketing campaign, I would look at my Google Analytics to see how many people had visited that page in the last few days. Over the month I could see which emails were the most popular. I knew that if I had a lot of website visits one day, say 120 visits, then the sales would roll in during the next few days. I also knew that if only 25 people had visited the site, then I probably wouldn't even get one sale.

As the database grew, so did the unsubscribe requests. It was often difficult to find the email address that I needed to remove. People often had a number of different email accounts. Sometimes they would send me an email requesting to be removed but the email was sent from a different email address. When this happened, I would have to email them back asking for their other email addresses as I couldn't find them on the system. Understandably, people were reluctant to provide further email addresses when all they wanted to do was remove the email address I had sent to. It was fine if they had replied to my email as I could see the email address that I had originally sent to but if they had created a new email, it caused me a problem.

In addition to this, I was getting upset by some of the comments. People would reply with the word 'remove' in the title and then add a few comments about how annoyed they were about receiving my email. Sometimes the language was very offensive. I couldn't blame them. I had emailed them without permission. I understood their point.

If somebody asked for their email address to be unsubcribed from my database, I had to make sure I did this within 14 days. As I tended to email weekly, I decided to remove their email address before the next email send. The last thing I wanted to do was send them another email and receive more upsetting emails. The process of removing the email addresses from my database was taking up to 4 hours a week. It was becoming unmanageable.

I also wanted to make sure that I did not re-add the email addresses to my database by mistake. It was difficult to keep track of all the email addresses. I was concerned that I would forget that I had previously collected the email addresses on a business website, and I would re-add the email addresses to my database by mistake. I would then be breaking the law. To prevent this I created a database of email addresses that had requested to be removed from my database.

I could see that my system was flawed and as the database grew I would have to spend more and more time removing email addresses manually. I decided that I needed to automate the system with an unsubscribe link. It didn't cost much, only about £130 at the time. It was great. From then on people could click the unsubscribe link and automatically be removed. The system kept their email address on file so even if I tried to add their email address to the system again, it would not allow me to do so.

## Telesales Using Own Database

To give myself a break from the email database, I decided to try selling my training courses over the telephone. I discovered that just as with email marketing, telesales had its own set of rules. In the UK there was a Telephone Preference Service (TPS). The TPS was a list that consumers and businesses could sign up to if they did not wish to be contacted by cold callers. If I wanted to call a business, I had to check whether or not they were on the TPS list. If they were on the list, I was not allowed to call them. I had to pay a small monthly fee to access this list.

After a few months of trying telesales, I had got nowhere. I hadn't made one sale. I found that most of the time it was difficult to get to speak to the person I needed to. If I did manage to speak to someone, they weren't interested in my product. I think, to be honest, I was pretty terrible at telesales. I decided to stop the telesales and cancelled my TPS subscription.

## Canvas Banner

After I had run a couple of training courses, I was preparing for my third training course. I needed a few more delegates to book places. As my father could make canvas banners, we thought it might be a good idea to create a banner in order to raise awareness of my training event. I knew banners worked as I had used them in my previous job when I was working as a counsellor. I had held a charity event and had put a banner up on the school gates for the month prior to the event. This was pretty much the only marketing I did. This event was really busy and hundreds of people had turned up.

The venue I had booked for my training course was in the city centre on one of the busiest roads. Buses were constantly passing the venue all the time so lots of people would see my banner. I asked permission from the venue who were more than happy for me to put the banner up. The banner was pretty large and hung on the black wrought iron railings. With its bright pink and yellow colours it was pretty impossible to miss. If I had paid for this banner it would have cost me about £100.

The banner was up for about two weeks prior to my event. Unfortunately, the banner didn't work and I didn't sell any more places on my course.

## Website Redesign With On-line Payment System

In 2010, I wanted to start offering on-line training courses. I needed my website to host the on-line courses, take payments and be capable of automatically emailing the customer with a link to their course once the payment had been accepted. The website needed a complete redesign. It cost me £2500. I didn't have this kind of money spare so had to borrow it.

I could not use a simple 'add to cart' shopping basket due to the functionality I required. This was one of the reasons the website cost so much to build. In order to take payments, I chose to use a merchant service from a high street bank.

Having this merchant service meant that I could also take payments over the telephone. This was great for me as I was dealing with large companies who often wanted to pay their invoices by card over the telephone.

The merchant service cost a minimum of £20 (plus VAT) a month. If I did not take any card payments in a month, I still had to pay the monthly fee as a minimum charge. If I took over a certain amount in card payments, I had to pay more than the £20 (plus VAT) monthly fee. This was fine when business was booming, but not so great when it was quieter. It doesn't sound much a month but over the year it cost at least £240 plus VAT.

The merchant services contract tied me in for a year. I learned that if I changed my business status from a sole trader to a limited company, I would have to have a new merchant account and would still remain in contract with the old account.

The provider of my merchant services would often email me and request that I update some element of the merchant services on my website. I very rarely understood these. I had to either speak to the merchant provider or my web developer to make sure that I was still compliant.

In addition to the merchant fees I also had to pass certain security checks as I was taking people's card details over the internet. I had to pay a £70 yearly fee to an online payment security company who would conduct a scan on my IP address every 3 months. I also had to complete self-assessment security questionnaires that I never really understood. The company talked me through them so I guessed everything was fine.

It took 6 months to redesign the website to incorporate the on-line courses and the payment system. My web developer did not have the technical know-how to implement the changes I required. He therefore informed me that he was using a subcontractor to help him.

Once the website was ready, I promoted the courses through my email marketing and they slowly started to sell. I also posted on

Linked In to announce the launch of the on-line courses. I am not sure if the Linked In post brought in any business.

## Price Points

Although the one day training courses and the on-line training courses were selling, I was yet to sell an in-house training course. My in-house training courses were designed for organisations who wanted a number of employees to attend one particular course. The training course would be delivered at their office and last for six hours.

When I first started offering training courses I had researched what other training companies were charging for in-house training courses. One trainer in my local area was selling a one day in-house training course, for 10 delegates, for £2500. I knew instantly that I could not achieve this. I was new to the field and had no reputation. I decided to go a bit cheaper and price my in-house course at £1850 for 12 delegates. From 2009-2011 I didn't sell any of these courses.

In 2012, I decided to reduce the price to £995 and the courses started to sell. I sold a total of 8 in-house courses in 2012.

People say if your products or services are too cheap, it will put people off. I believe this can certainly be the case but if you price yourself too highly you can risk not making any sales at all. I should have realised I was too expensive a lot sooner.

## Fine Tuning The Unsolicited Email Marketing

At this stage a few more people had signed up to my email list via the sign up form on my website. I now had about 50 subscribers. Clearly this was still a very small number so I continued with the unsolicited business-to-business email marketing.

I read various books on email marketing but for me it was trial and error. In the beginning, my email subject titles were very general. For example, I would title the email 'CPD Training Courses' which basically meant training courses for Continuing Professional Development, which lots of professions require (solicitors, accountants, teachers etc.). When I was using general titles the email marketing would result in a few sales. One day I decided to advertise a specific product instead. This time I titled the email 'The Psychology of Conflict Resolution'. The sales rocketed. From then on, I usually advertised a single product in the email title. I switched the products around and advertised a different product each time. As soon as I veered off this rule with a title like 'On-line Training Courses' the sales would drastically slow down.

Many of the books I read on email marketing told me to send my emails on certain days to maximise the impact. I found this was true to a certain extent. Sending my emails on a Monday or a Friday resulted in significantly less sales. I guessed this was because on a Monday people were really busy. They were probably too busy to read and absorb their emails. On a Friday people were relaxed and winding down for the weekend. Come the following Monday my email would be long forgotten. I settled on sending on a Tuesday evening. This worked well for me for many years. In the end I had about 120 000 people in my database so it used to take me a couple of days to send to my full list.

I also had to consider how often to send the email marketing. The email marketing books I read said that if you email once a month, people will forget about you. They usually advised to send email marketing once a fortnight. I found weekly worked well for me. Sending the emails fortnightly or monthly didn't bring in enough business.

The email marketing books suggested that email marketing should contain interesting content that people care about. I started to write newsletters with the latest psychological research. The newsletters took me about a day to write. Whenever I sent out the newsletters I would receive sarcastic comments about the research. On the weeks that I sent out the newsletters, instead of adverts, I received barely any sales as a result. In the end I stopped writing the newsletters and just sent out adverts week after week.

Email marketing wasn't always a smooth process. Although I liked the sales it brought in, I didn't actually like sending the email marketing. I disliked receiving unwanted emails myself and here I was sending them out to others. I started to dread Tuesday nights when I had to hit the send button on the email marketing campaign. I would regularly receive emails from people calling me all sorts of names for being a 'spammer'. Although I technically wasn't a spammer, it still made me feel uncomfortable. On one occasion I even had a man phone me up and physically threaten me. He said that if I sent another email to him he would come and beat me up! As I ran my business from home and had my home address on my website, I felt pretty upset by this. When I spoke to people about the negative comments, people told me that I just needed 'to grow a thicker skin'. I wanted to stop the email marketing, but without the email marketing I didn't have a business.

At one point my emails stopped arriving. My customers, suppliers and business contacts were not receiving my emails. I had also noticed that my sales had dropped in the last few weeks. The email marketing was not having its usual impact. I could not figure out what was wrong and contacted my web developer. He said that I was on a blacklist. My email marketing had been flagged as spam.

Even though my email marketing was technically not spam, it had been flagged as spam. My web developer informed me that a number of people must have flagged my emails as spam and therefore I had been added to a blacklist. The blacklist company considered me a spammer and therefore would block my future emails.

My web developer contacted the blacklist company and explained that I was doing business-to-business email marketing. He informed the blacklist company that I was following all the legal requirements for the UK. The company said they would remove me from the blacklist list in the next 48 hours. I was so relieved.

I started sending the email marketing again and within a few months my emails stopped arriving again. This time I searched the Internet and found that I could check for myself if my domain was listed on any blacklists. I typed in my domain name and found that it was once again listed on some blacklists. When I looked at the blacklist websites, they provided instructions for removing my domain name from their lists. I had to email them explaining my email marketing processes. I followed the instructions and they removed my domain name from their list. The blacklist companies usually offered to remove my domain name from their list within 48 hours. Some of the companies offered to do it quicker than this but for a £20 to £30 fee.

I started to doubt myself and wondered if I was actually breaking the law. I needed some reassurance so called the Information Commissioner's Office in the UK once again. I spoke with an advisor who reassured me that I was not breaking any UK laws. I also emailed the Information Commissioner's Office with the same question as I wanted the answer in writing.

The blacklist issue was proving to be a bit of a problem. I needed to reduce the likelihood of it happening again. I decided to put a note at the bottom of my email marketing quoting the legal legislation for business-to-business email marketing in the UK. I hoped that my note explaining that I was within my legal rights to email them would prevent some people from reporting me as spam.

This seemed to help. Although my domain name was occasionally added to a blacklist, most of the time my emails got through to people's inboxes.

For years, email marketing worked brilliantly for my business. It was the only marketing that worked and it was pretty cheap. I was not using an email marketing provider at this point (I'll talk about these later), as they were too expensive. Instead I had set up a dedicated server through a hosting company and used that to send my emails. Through the dedicated server I was allowed to send 3600 emails an hour. They didn't request that the emails were opt-in, so I could email businesses freely.

By 2013, business was really busy. I employed six subcontractors across the UK to deliver one day training courses on an 'as and when' basis. I also had to hire a part-time administrative assistant to help me cope with my workload.

The email marketing alone was providing me with a £120,000 turnover. For those of you who are unsure of the term 'turnover', it simply means how much I sold in total in a year. It is not the same as profit. Profit is the turnover figure minus expenses.

My web designer and business coach persistently warned me that I needed to find a different way to market my business. They said that at some point I would be permanently blacklisted and would not be able to send my emails. I had this at the back of my mind, but so far I had managed to use email marketing since 2009 to 2013. It hadn't happened so far and I wondered if it would ever happen.

As business was going so well in 2013, I felt that all I needed to do was keep adding email addresses to my email list and the business would keep growing. I figured that if I could add another 120 000 email addresses to my list over the next few years, I could double my turnover from £120,000 to £240,000.

The only thing that kept me trying different marketing methods in 2013 was the fact that I disliked sending the unsolicited email marketing. I hoped that I would find an alternative way to market the business.

## Posting Flyers Nationally

I decided to try posting flyers again. This time I wanted to try advertising the in-house courses. The in-house courses were selling fairly well and I figured that I could direct the flyers to the HR managers of various companies across the UK.

I had the flyers professionally printed this time as I wanted to use a photo on the flyer, with a glossy finish. I ordered 100 flyers initially. I sent out an initial 50 flyers and got no interest. I gave up at this point and left the rest of the flyers in the drawer.

## Social Media Marketing With Twitter

I started to feel like I was running out of marketing ideas. I hadn't yet tried social media marketing so decided to try this next.

I liked the idea of using Twitter to market my business and bought an eBook which promised to help me get thousands of followers.

The book advised that I should firstly locate my competitors on Twitter. Once I had done this, I needed to look through their list of followers and then follow all of their followers.

The book suggested that if I followed someone on Twitter, they may feel compelled to follow me back out of politeness. I followed this advice and to my amazement it worked. Within three months I had reached 1000 followers.

I used an app to help monitor my followers. It automatically unfollowed someone when they did not follow me back within 14 days. I found this was a great tool as it reduced the number of people I was following.

After some time I decided to unfollow everyone. I think at the time I thought it would make my business look more popular if I was following virtually no one, yet had 1000 followers. Overnight I lost about 140 followers. I suspect that these users had an app which automatically unfollowed anyone who unfollowed them.

The Twitter marketing book suggested that I should market to my followers on a 10:2 ratio. This meant that in every 10 tweets I sent, only 2 of these should be marketing. It also suggested that I should re-tweet other people's tweets in the hope that they will then re-tweet my tweets. The book advised adding popular trending hash tags to my tweets to help people find me.

I spent about four months trying to sell through twitter and didn't manage to sell anything. I think it may have been because my followers were mainly businesses. I suspect that these businesses employed someone to manage the company's twitter account and this person had no purchasing power. I did market to some individuals too but perhaps they were happy with my competitors and felt no need to change.

## Using A Search Engine Optmisation Company

I was still looking for an alternative way to market my products and turned my attention back to Search Engine Optimisation. I really wanted to try and get higher up in the Google search results. I met with a friend of my sisters who had used a foreign company who provided SEO relatively cheaply. I had tried to do the SEO work myself and had failed. I felt it was time to employ a company who knew what they were doing.

The SEO company asked for my top ten keywords. They informed me that I would receive progress reports each month. The reports would notify me of my position in the search engine results for each of my ten keywords.

At the time, all links in to a website were really important. The SEO company were basically registering my business and website on lots of different directories. They were also writing short blog posts which included links to various pages on my website.

At £130 a month, the SEO work was not particularly cheap. However, if I was using a company in the UK, I think it would have been considerably more expensive. I decided I needed to make this investment and if I could get on first page Google (as they promised) then business would come rolling in. I figured it would be worth the investment.

After a few months, the company started sending me the reports. My website did appear a little higher in the search results, but not high enough to make any difference. I was on about page three or four of Google search results for most of my keywords.

After about 4 to 5 months, I had moved further up the search results. My website now appeared either at the bottom of page two or the top of page three for most of my keyword searches.

After another 4 months, my website had not moved much higher in the search results. I felt that I was just throwing money away. The SEO company could not tell me how much longer it would take for my website to appear on the first page of the search results. My competitors who were appearing higher on the search results were large corporations. I felt that I wasn't going to get much higher in the search results and stopped the SEO work.

It was years ago now that I spent the money on the SEO work, yet people are still finding my website via Google. At the moment I probably get about 20 visits a month from Google searches which admittedly, compared to other websites, is a small amount. In terms of sales I probably make a sale once every couple of months via the search traffic. Usually the sale is a one hour on-line course which these days costs £12.50 but sometimes it's a company account costing about £400.

## Advertising On A Business Directory On A National Newspaper's Website

I was still keen to find another way to market my products. At the time, one of the national papers in the UK were offering to advertise training courses on their training course directory for £1000. My advert would appear in the directory for one year. Although it was a lot of money, I felt confident that I would receive sales from it. I was really excited to be advertising with a national newspaper.

During the whole year, I sold one training course. Unfortunately, the person who booked the training course had to cancel at short notice and did not rebook.

## Advertising On An Industry Specific On-line Business Directory With Commission Only Agreement

During 2012, I added my training courses to another business directory for training courses. This business directory was different in that I did not have to pay any upfront marketing fees. When one of my courses sold, the company took the full payment from the customer and sent me an email with the order details. I then supplied the training course to the customer and a month later the company made direct payment into my bank account. This payment was the total sale amount minus their commission. I have found the commission on these types of sites vary. In my experience they can vary from 20% to 60% commission.

I really liked advertising with this company due to the fact they offered a commission only agreement. There was no risk for me whatsoever. If I didn't sell anything, I didn't get charged. This site has made me about £150 a year since I started using it. Obviously, this isn't a great deal of money, but it is still £150 profit I would not have otherwise made.

## Telesales Using An Industry Specific Business Directory

I found a business directory that listed a number of different companies with the contact name of the person responsible for purchasing training. This business directory was updated every year and every training contact listed had agreed that people could contact them with a telesales call regarding training. This meant I did not need to have the Telephone Preference List membership.

The directory was fairly expensive at £140 but I figured I only needed to make a few sales to get my money back. There were thousands of businesses listed. I would never make it through all of them.

I felt I wasn't very good at telesales and decided to hire a telesales company to make the calls for me. I was already using a company to answer my telephone calls when I was busy and knew they offered a telesales service. I met with the manager to explain my products in detail. I had decided that I wanted to focus on selling company subscriptions to the on-line courses as these were the easiest to sell. We went through the telesales pitch and I felt confident the manager understood my products and my business. The telesales company created a script and I provided the telesales team with a list of businesses to start working through. I initially provided the team with a list of 130 businesses. I figured that as I started to see the sales roll in, I would provide them with another list of businesses to call. I felt confident the telesales team would make some sales.

The team started to call through the database. At the end of each day they would send me the database list together with their notes. It struck me that the named contact in the business directory often claimed to have nothing to do with training decisions. This pattern continued and the telesales team were finding it very difficult to speak to the person they needed to. They were constantly fobbed off and told to call back at various times. After about 8 weeks of the telesales work, at 14 hours a week, I decided to stop it. I hadn't made a single sale and there weren't any warm leads to follow up on.

## The Demise Of The Unsolicited Email Marketing

Towards the end of 2013 I noticed that my email marketing wasn't really working anymore. I was sending the emails week after week but the sales had virtually stopped. My emails weren't getting through to customers either. This had been happening for a few months and I could not understand what was happening. Interestingly, when I looked at the blacklists, my domain was not blacklisted.

I had to try and understand what was happening. For a few solid weeks I aimlessly searched the Internet. Eventually, I found a website designed for web developers. I used their search facility and it identified that I was in fact blacklisted. I was blacklisted with a company that had only recently started trading and this was why it was not appearing on the other blacklist searches.

I found the company's website and looked through the information on their site. Their company aim was to stop all bulk unsolicited email. They recognised that whilst companies were within their legal rights to send bulk unsolicited business-to-business emails, they wanted the web to be a place where this did not happen. This company was different to the other blacklisting companies; the other blacklisting companies were solely aiming to stop illegal activities whereas this company were aiming to stop legal activities too.

I asked for my domain to be removed from their list and it was removed within a day. The next week I sent an email marketing message out to my database list of 120 000 email addresses. I noticed within 3 hours of hitting the send button that my emails had stopped arriving. I went on to their website and checked my domain name. It had been blocked already. I had not even finished sending my email marketing campaign.

I wondered if I was blacklisted again because the blacklisting company were now keeping an eye on my domain. I asked to be removed from the list and they removed me once again. Their website stated that they would only remove a domain name twice, before they would refuse all future requests and the domain name would remain permanently on their black list.

The next week, I sent the email marketing via an alternative domain name on a new dedicated server. Once again within about 5 hours of sending the emails, I noticed the emails were not arriving. I checked the blacklisting company's website and my new domain name was listed on their blacklist.

It seemed as soon as I sent out any bulk unsolicited email, I would be instantly blacklisted from now on. If I continued to send the emails, I would be permanently blacklisted.

This was a really tough time for me. Email marketing was the only way I could make my business work. I felt upset and angry that this company had set up and were allowed to stop my perfectly legal emails from arriving. I felt they had effectively ruined my business. Without my business, I was going to struggle financially. I had literally just bought my first house and taken out a mortgage.

I could understand why people would want to use their service. I appreciated that people didn't like receiving unsolicited emails and wanted to use spam filters to stop them.

My web developer and business coach had been right after all. They always said that the spam filters would get stronger and one day I would find myself permanently blacklisted.

I had no choice but to stop all unsolicited email marketing. I made the decision to switch to double opt-in email marketing and send through a recognised email marketing service to make sure that my emails would arrive.

## Double Opt-In Email Marketing

From now on I was going to use double opt-in email marketing only. Double opt-in required a person to first sign up to my email list and then reconfirm via their email that they wanted to be added to my list.

Firstly, I considered sending the double opt-in emails myself. However, I wondered how a blacklisting company would know that people had double-opted in to my emails. As soon as I started sending to a large number of email addresses again, I was sure I would run in to blacklisting problems once again.

I decided that I needed to use an email marketing provider. These companies have a high deliverability rate. This means that virtually everybody on my email list would receive my emails. As these companies only send to people who have opted-in, they have a good reputation with the spam filters.

I researched the deliverability rates for the different email marketing providers and chose the one with the highest deliverability rates. I wanted to make sure my subscriber's emails landed in their inboxes and not their junk/spam folders. I got my first month free and then had to pay a monthly subscription based on the number of subscribers I had. I noticed from their tariff page that the more subscribers I had, the more expensive the monthly fee. I also noticed that I would be charged a monthly fee even if I did not send out any emails within the month. Out of interest I looked at the monthly cost for 120 000 subscribers. It was expensive. If I ever reached this number of subscribers, I would have to seriously look at the costs of the email marketing and the subsequent profit it resulted in.

The email marketing provider offered a number of free professionally designed email templates. All I had to do was add my own words and images to create a professional looking email marketing message. Previously I only had one template for my emails and I had used this same template every week. It was nice to have a number of different templates to choose from. Each email automatically had my organisation address and an unsubscribe link at the bottom.

I was able to preview my email and send myself a test version. This allowed me to look at the email on different systems such as a laptop computer and a mobile.

I could also set up auto responders. I set up an auto responder for new subscribers. Any new subcriber would receive an automatic email from me which thanked them for signing up and informed them how often they could expect to receive my emails.

When I sent out my first email marketing campaign to my subscribers, I noticed that I could analyse how my email performed. I could look at which subscribers opened my email and who clicked on the links and visited my website.

There was also a section of the email marketing analysis which showed how many people reported the emails as spam. After sending my first email marketing through this system, I noticed that one person had reported me as spam. I was confused how this could be the case when the person had double opted-in to receive my emails. I looked through the help topics on the email marketing provider's website and they stated that it is fairly common as people can forget they signed up to your email list.

**Building The Opt-In Email Marketing List**

Ever since the business started I had been trying to grow my opt-in email list. By this time I had about 120 people on my subscriber list. I imported them into the email marketing provider's website and confirmed they had previously double opted-in via an alternative site. At this stage in the business, I usually got about one sign up every two months. Now I had stopped the unsolicited email marketing completely, I needed to build my opt-in email marketing list quickly.

I emailed all of my previous clients and offered them a free on-line course if they signed up to my email list. I received about 120 responses in total.

I tried asking various community and business newsletters if I could offer the same deal to their readership. One business newsletter, who I had worked with in the past, said I could put an advert in the newsletter for free. I put an advert in their newsletter and received about another 5 sign ups. Getting people to opt-in to my email marketing was a slow process.

I researched how to increase my number of opt-in subscribers. I paid £30 for a document which promised to show me how to build my subscriber list. It stated that I could get 5000 subscribers in just a few weeks. I thought 'great, this is just what I need'. The document was generally not very helpful and most of the techniques were common sense. However, it did recommend using a pop-up form on my website that asked people to sign up to the newsletter. I looked into doing this and within a week I had a pop-up sign up form on my website.

I set the pop-up to appear after a person had been on my website for 10 seconds. I felt this gave them a chance to have a short look at the site before asking them to sign up. The pop-up form was set to appear once every ten times a customer visited the site.

I knew some people would find my pop-up annoying but I wanted to see if it increased the number of subscribers. As soon as I put it on the website, I started to receive notifications every week that people had signed up to my newsletter. I have now been collecting email addresses, using a pop-up form, for a year and a half. I now have about 550 people signed up to my opt-in email list.

## Results Of My Opt-in Email Marketing

I emailed the subscribers a number of times but didn't receive any sales as a result. I believed this was because it was a numbers game. I needed a lot more subscribers.

The email marketing analysis tools made it easy to see how many people unsubscribed from my list each time I sent a marketing email. I usually had 1 or 2 people unsubscribe. I did send out one particular email and had a surge of people unsubscribe. I had started offering a private counselling service and sent this information out to my list of subscribers. I had about 13 people unsubscribe that day. Due to the high number of unsubscribers I decided not to send that email advert again.

My research on email marketing highlighted that opt-in subscribers were more likely to purchase products compared to people who received unsolicited emails. This was because they had already expressed an interest in the products and the business.

Although the double opt-in email marketing wasn't working for me, I believed it could in the future if I could obtain enough subscribers. I decided that all I could do was to keep on growing the list steadily and hope that it would start to produce some sales in the future.

As I had not made any sales, I switched to an alternative email marketing provider with a slightly lower deliverability rate. I switched because for my low number of subscribers they offered the same service for no monthly fee.

## Website Blog

I had heard that blogs were a great way to market a business for free. I knew that I could either have a blog on my website or use a free blogger site.

I started to research blogging on the Internet. It seemed that all I had to do was write interesting content for my blog, and people would find the blog via web searches and word of mouth. Once people were reading my blog, I could then direct them to my product pages on my website.

Blogging sounded like a great idea to me, especially because it would only cost my time to try it. I decided to use the blog on my own website. This was mainly because I wanted the content on my site. I had already written a few blog posts years ago and figured that even if the blogging didn't work, I would at least have some more of my keywords on the website for SEO purposes.

I was hoping that my blog would either lead to sales or at least a few sign ups to my opt-in email list. I decided to add a 'sign up to our newsletter' box at the end of each blog post.

I started writing my blog posts. I felt they were interesting posts that my target audience would want to read. I wrote one a week for about 2 months.

I tried advertising my blog on social media sites and tying it in with trending hash tags. Whenever I did this, it usually resulted in one or two views on my blog.

Perhaps I did not keep going long enough, but the blogs didn't achieve anything. I received no sales and no one signed up to my newsletter via the blog. I think the biggest problem was that no one knew my blog existed as it did not show up in any search engine results.

**Social Media Marketing With Facebook**

At the time I kept hearing how great Facebook was for advertising small businesses. My page was not very popular even though I linked to it from my website and at the end of each of my on-line courses. At the time I only had about 15 likes.

I decided to create a paid ad to promote the on-line courses. I only set a budget of about £12. I wanted to set a higher budget but now I had stopped the unsolicited email marketing I was only selling a few on-line courses a month.

I promoted my post to people with an interest in Human Resources in the UK. I felt HR professionals were the most likely to purchase my products. I received about 8 likes on the post. I did not sell any on-line courses and did not receive any extra page likes.

At the time I spoke to some friends about my experiences of advertising on Facebook. They suggested that people tended to go on to Facebook for pleasure not business. It was their free time and probably the last thing they wanted to do was think about work and potential training courses.

## Advertising In Magazines

I was still looking for another way to market the business. I had always wanted to advertise in a business magazine and decided to look in to the costs.

I made enquiries to a few business magazines. The magazines wanted about a £1000 for one advert. In addition to this, I had to purchase three adverts as a minimum order.

The magazines advised me that I would need to advertise three times in order for somebody to make a purchase. One magazine told me that when a potential customer sees the advert for the first time, they think 'that's a good idea, I must do something about it' but ultimately they forget about the advert. When they see the advert a second time, they think 'oh yes, I forgot about that and I really should do something about it this time' and once again they forget. When they see the advert a third time, they think 'right, I'll do something about this right now' and they will make a purchase.

I had heard that people actually needed to see an advert 6-8 times and in different mediums (email, magazine advert, post) before they made a purchase. I had no idea how many times a person actually had to see an advert before they made a purchase. I thought back to when I was sending the unsolicited email marketing. Some people would purchase a course the first time they received my email marketing whereas others would make their first purchase after a few years of receiving my weekly emails.

I thought the magazines were probably right. A single advert might not result in many sales. However, I wasn't willing or able to risk £3000 on advertising in a magazine.

## Marketing Advice Book

At this point in the business I really started to panic. I had stopped the unsolicited email marketing about 6 months prior and I still hadn't found an alternative way to successfully market the business. I was beginning to wonder whether I would have to look for a job. I knew finding a job would be difficult as I needed to be able to work from home due to a long standing health problem. The thought of giving up my business after nearly seven years worth of work was unbearable. I loved my business and loved being my own boss. In desperation I decided to look for a marketing book. I hoped there was still a chance that I could learn how to successfully market my business.

I found a marketing book specifically for small businesses. The reviews were great. They were nearly all positive. Many reviewers claimed they had implemented the tools in the book and had received extra sales as a result. I was filled with confidence. I just had to follow the book's instructions and I could get my business back on track.

When I usually read business books, I tended to skim over the exercises thinking they would make no real difference. I only took on board the learning points that I agreed with. Well this approach hadn't worked very well in the past so this time I was going to approach things differently. I would do all of the exercises and follow all of the advice. I went to the local stationers and bought myself a new highlighter pen, a new writing pen, a gold A4 leaver arch folder and a pad of lined paper. I was going to give this book my best shot.

As soon as I started reading the book, I was hooked. Everything the writer said made complete sense to me.

## Copy Changes

The book made me realise that I needed to change the way I had worded my marketing on my website. I had written the product description all about the product, rather than writing it TO the potential customer. So for my conflict resolution course, my website currently just listed the content of the training course. This book advised that I needed to rewrite this as if I was talking to the customer. For example, 'Do you want to manage the difficult people in your life more effectively? Would you like to know the right thing to say in an argument?'

I liked this idea and spent the next month working through the many pages of my website. I changed everything according to her advice. I even changed one of my web page titles. The original page title was 'In-House Training Courses'. I wanted the title to more obviously reflect the product I was offering and changed it to 'Our Courses - Your Offices'. Overnight I saw this page become far more popular. It had an extra 20 clicks on it in just a few days.

I was really pleased with all the changes I had made. The website was much more inviting. I felt that people would be able to instantly see how the course could improve their working life. I felt sure that this would ultimately result in more sales.

## Price Checking

The other good piece of advice this book gave me was to regularly check the price that my competitors were charging. I was charging £25 per on-line course and as far as I knew I was competitively priced. I had checked my competitors prices a few years ago when I first started offering the on-line training. I figured the price might have gone up but was happy to continue offering the courses for £25.

On the advice of this book, I decided to check my competitors prices. I felt sure that the prices would not have changed and I was just going through the motions in order to prove myself right. In fact, I discovered that the prices had halved. The average price now was only £12.50. No wonder I was finding sales difficult when I was twice the price!

Within a week of publishing the word changes and new prices on my website, I made two sales. I couldn't believe it! I hadn't sold anything in months. I thought to myself 'wow, that really did make a difference' I started telling my friends and family what a difference it had made, and how I hoped that my business would be back on track now. I felt confident that people landing on the website would now be more likely to buy the courses.

Turns out I was celebrating victory too soon. Sadly, these two sales were flukes. Ultimately, my sales did not increase as a result of changing my wording and my prices. It had made no difference at all.

## Sales Letters

The book suggested sending potential customers a sales letter. The author said sales letters worked because people didn't receive many letters these days. She argued that marketing emails would disappear in a plethora of other people's emails. I was slightly reluctant to follow the advice as posting flyers had not worked for me previously.

However, I had tried posting flyers but not sales letters. The book gave examples of sales letters that the author had personally helped to write. Each of the sales letters had been successful.

At the very top of each letter, the company had written a snappy summary of what they were offering. The letter would then go on to explain the benefits of the product or service and how they were different to competitors.

The companies had usually sent out about 50 letters to potential customers. The author reported that some of the sales letters had resulted in a 25% success rate. 25% of people who had received the letter had called the business to make an order. This was without any further marketing action such as a follow up sales call or email. Other sales letters had received similar results. I studied the sales letters meticulously.

I thought I had created the perfect sales letter to sell my annual subscriptions to my online courses. I structured it similar to the example sales letters. The author recommended that after I had written the letter, I should review it and re-draft it at least a couple of times. I followed the advice. I showed it to a number of people and reviewed it about 6 times to make sure it stood the best chance.

The book was very particular and stated that I should use a high quality, cream envelope. The paper should also be high quality. I went out and bought 50 quality envelopes at the expense of £7. I already had some good quality paper. Of course I also had to buy 50 stamps. The author recommended using first class stamps in order to look professional. I followed every single piece of her advice.

To decide who to send the sales letters to, I needed to conduct an analysis of my previous sales. I collated a database of all my previous customers. I analysed the type of company who tended to purchase my products. I looked at the position of the purchaser, organisation sector, organisation size and their location. My analysis showed the customers who bought my online training courses were usually from smaller companies and I had usually dealt directly with the manager or the director.

The book had also mentioned that when I was deciding who to market to, I should go for the path of least resistance. It mentioned that it might be easier to sell to smaller companies where you can market directly to the manager as opposed to larger companies who employed secretaries to filter the post and phone calls. I thought this was good advice.

I decided to target small companies partly because of the authors advice and partly because it tended to be small businesses who purchased my online courses. Most of my clients were solicitors so I decided to target small solicitor firms, with less than 10 employees.

By the time I posted my letter I had spent two months incorporating the lessons from this book. I had reworded my website, researched and changed my prices and sent out a beautifully crafted sales letter. By this stage I was convinced that my sales letter would work.

I sent the letters feeling full of hope and waited a few days until they had arrived. I can remember making sure I stayed in all day for the next few days as I was convinced the phone would ring. Unfortunately the phone never rang.

The author advised that a follow up phone call a week after sending the sales letter would further boost sales. If I had got some initial sales from the sales letters, I might have felt encouraged to make some follow-up phone calls. But as I had not made any sales I decided not to bother. This was partly because I felt the sales letter hadn't worked and partly because I had never found telesales to work for my business.

I knew that emails had worked for me in the past and so decided that I would send a follow up email instead. I figured I would not get blacklisted as I was only sending 50 or so emails. I managed to find email addresses for the managers or directors of two thirds of the companies. I sent out the emails and received a couple of responses. Unfortunately, they were just polite refusals. No sales ever came as a result of this sales letter. I was really disappointed.

I felt deterred but still had a few things to try as a result of this book. Perhaps something else would work. After all, if it had worked for everyone else, there was no reason that it shouldn't work for me and my business.

## Targeted Email Marketing To Previous Customers

The next marketing effort was to send a marketing message to a different select group of people as a result of the analysis of my previous customer base.

As emails had previously worked for my business, I decided I would send emails. Rather than sending unsolicited emails to potential

60

customers, I wanted to send emails to previous customers asking if they would like to purchase an annual subscription for the on-line courses. I sent about 300 emails over the course of 4 weeks.

I then discovered that my emails had stopped arriving. I did a blacklist search and found that once again I was on a blacklist. I had only sent 300 emails and each one was personalised to that company. My web developer read the email that I had sent and felt that it was a 'little spammy', but he was surprised that it had got my domain black listed.

We managed to get my domain removed from the blacklist. At this point I decided that I would not send any more unsolicited emails of any kind.

## Marketing Advice Book Results

After following the advice in the marketing book for 3 solid months, I had achieved nothing. I had followed the advice exactly and it had not worked. I was really surprised. I wondered if the reason the advice didn't work for me was because my products were too niche.

## Using Other Industry Specific On-line Directories With Commission Only Agreements

Marketing experts often say 'do more of what works'. At the end of 2013, apart from receiving the odd purchase via a Google search, the only marketing that was working for my business was selling my courses on a business directory website, with a commission only agreement. Advertising on this one site was making me a small profit of £150 a year.

As this method of advertising was working, I decided to see if I could find similar sites to advertise my courses on. I only wanted to advertise on websites where there were no upfront costs. I was happy for the company to take a percentage if they sold something for me but I didn't want to pay them if they failed to sell anything.

I found an American site which offered a commission only agreement. I signed up and learned that I needed to upload my courses to their site. I had to put each course into a different format and with 26 courses this was no small job. I spent about two weeks converting all the courses and making sure they worked correctly on their system. The courses have been up for about 2 years now and they have made me about £40 profit.

I also contacted another on-line business directory who sold training courses. It did not state that they offered advertising on a commission only basis so I emailed their head office on the off-chance. About 3 months later I received a phone call from their head office stating that they had kept my email on file as it was a new service they were going to offer in the future. My courses were subsequently listed on their website and I started to receive sales from the site every month.

## Discount Voucher Sites

I was searching for similar business directory sites to add my courses to when I landed on a discount voucher website. I read the information on their website and realised that they worked on a commission only basis. This was just what I was looking for.

I completed the on-line application form but received an email a week later saying that my product was not right for their customers. I applied to a few more discount voucher sites and my applications were declined.

About 6 months later, I was searching the Internet again and found another discount voucher site to apply to. I entered my contact details and to my surprise they contacted me back. I had to speak with their head office over the telephone to discuss the deal. They suggested an amount to discount my product by and I was happy with their suggestion. The discount voucher site informed me of their commission rates. The rates were fairly high but I could still make a profit on each item sold. The deal was agreed and I was sent the contracts to sign. The deal was created and the draft documents were sent through to me. I was really pleased with how the company had worded my advert. It sounded superb.

I needed to amend my website in order to be able to accept the voucher codes. My web developer told me he didn't know how to put this functionality on my website. He suggested that I liaise directly with the subcontractor he had been using.

The subcontractor added the new functionality and it all appeared to work fine. I paid him his fee. In the following weeks, I noticed that the new functionality was not actually working correctly. It was failing to update an important database. I contacted the subcontractor and he tried to fix it. However it still did not work. He tried to fix it a few more times without success and in the end he stopped responding to my messages.

I tried to find someone who would finish the work for me. I searched a website where you can employ freelancers to complete specific jobs. I posted the job description and received a few quotes. The first freelancer told me that my website was poorly made. He tried to fix the problem but when I tested the website, the database was still not updating. I messaged him back a few times but never heard anything more from him. Fortunately, I had not paid him upfront. I tried one more freelancer on the website.

He also told me that my website was poorly made and due to this fact he wasn't able to fix the problem.

I then went to a local web designer who I had known for years as they had previously done all of my printing. Once again I was told that the coding of my website was a mess. Now three people had told me this, I had to believe it. I was really disappointed. I had paid £2500 for a website that was poorly made and difficult to work on.

However, this web company had a team of expert web developers and although it wasn't easy to work on the site, they managed to fix the problem. I guess you get what you pay for. In total, having new functionality added to the website so that I could accept the discount voucher codes cost me about £380.

Now my website was able to accept the voucher codes, my deal was scheduled to start running about 14 days later. I was really excited and started to tell my family and friends. I can remember telling my sister the details of the deal and she said 'Wow, Lou! You are going to be a millionaire.' I thought I might be too! The first morning it went live, I looked at the sales. I was selling one deal every few minutes. I went cold. I thought this is it. I have found the answer. I'm going to be a millionaire at this rate. This was until 30 minutes later and the sales slowed right down.

The deal was live for a trial period. My product had to perform well in this time in order for the deal to remain on the site and be offered to a larger audience. Fortunately, I hit their targets and my contract was renewed.

Now my courses were on the discount voucher site, I had two other discount voucher sites contact me to ask if they could also sell my courses. Due to my contract with the current discount voucher site, I was unable to accept. However, I had developed some new courses and decided to trial the new courses on a different discount voucher website in order to compare the level of sales. The new discount voucher site wanted to offer the vouchers slightly differently so I had to amend the website once again. I needed to add the original functionality to a few new pages on the website. I asked my web developer to complete the work and within a few hours I had the functionality ready for the new discount voucher site. I figured it must have been a simple job of copying and pasting the code as it had been done so quickly and they had not quoted me a price. However, a month later I received an invoice for £180.

The deal went live on the new discount voucher site and I sold about £350 worth of products. This deal was only live for two weeks. I was pleased with the sales and would have been happy to run the deal again, however the discount voucher site said the sales were not high enough and therefore they would not be running the offer again.

The new courses were then added to the original discount voucher site. They were much less popular than my original courses but I still made sales on them every few days.

Advertising my products on the discount voucher site was also a great way to build my email list. People often visited my website before deciding to purchase the course through the discount voucher site. The pop-up sign up form encouraged them to subscribe. I usually obtained one new subscriber every other day.

As a side note, a year after using the freelancers who worked on my website, I had to copy and paste some text from one of the web pages into a Word document. I noticed that my pasted text had lots of links to on-line casinos and Viagra. Confused, I looked back at the web page. Nothing there. I then switched from viewing 'text' to viewing 'HTML' and there in the HTML were lots of links to various dodgy sites. I checked the other web pages and sure enough my site was littered with them. When I spoke to my new web developers they said that these links were written in white so they were invisible. They had been there for at least a year. I just hope no customers had copy and pasted text from my site in this time. My web developers said that I should have changed my password as soon as the freelancers had finished working on the site. I changed my password and removed all the links.

## Stalls At Events

At this stage, some of my marketing ideas were working but my turnover was still nowhere near what it used to be. I still needed to try and boost my sales.

I spoke to a friend of mine who was in the senior management team at a University. I asked him how he found the training courses that he subsequently booked. He said he only booked training courses via the stalls at conferences. Interestingly, he said he never booked courses via telesales calls or email marketing messages.

I decided to look into the cost of having a stall at a conference. The prices varied for the different conferences in my sector. The cheapest price was about £2000. I would have to sell a lot of training courses to make this a viable option. I wasn't convinced that my stall would be successful due to my experiences of running stalls in a previous job. £2000 was a lot of money to lose and I didn't want to risk it.

## Double Opt-In Email Database Lists For Sale

As email marketing was previously one of the best ways to sell my products, I decided to look into it once again. My opt-in list was still very small, and I hardly ever emailed the subscribers as it never resulted in any sales.

I searched the Internet and found a well known company who offered email data lists together with an email sending service. This seemed to answer all of my problems. The people on this list were double opt-in, and the company would send the emails so I would not be at risk of being blocked for spamming.

I had a discussion with their sales team. To send 12 500 emails, once a month, for three months, it was going to cost me £4000. I asked if I could send to less than 12 500 people and they informed me that they would not send to less than 10 000 people at a time.

I asked them why and they said that if 10 000 people received my email and I had a 10% open rate, 1000 people would have opened the email. If 5000 people received my email and I had a 10% open rate, only 500 people would have opened my email and therefore I might not receive a sale.

For me, the figures didn't work. My products mostly had a low price point and if I was only going to sell a few, I would be thousands of pounds out of pocket!

# The Business 2015

At present, the only marketing I use for the business is the training business directories and the discount voucher sites. These sites provide me with sales almost daily. I also still receive the odd sale from people finding the business via Google.

I plan to continue to grow my double opt-in email list and hope it will start to result in some sales as the list grows. I will need to keep an eye on the subscriber numbers as once I have a certain number of subscribers, I will start incurring monthly fees. If the monthly fees outweigh the sales from the email marketing, then I may have to close my account.

I have spent a lot of time recently talking to other professionals in various fields. They are all experiencing similar problems with marketing their small business. It seems that each company has spent a lot of time and money trialling different marketing initiatives.

Obviously, this book is just my experience of marketing a small business. I hope it has helped you in some way. I wanted to tell the truth about marketing a small business. The truth can be hard to come by when businesses are trying to keep up appearances and ensure others see them as successful.

Thank you for reading this book. If you have any questions, comments, or would like to share your marketing experiences, please feel free to contact me on
www.facebook.com/louisepalmerauthor

I love to hear from readers and will always reply to messages.

**More books by this author**

How to Manage Teams: The No Waffle Guide to Managing Your Team Effectively

Presentation Skills: Portraying Confidence, Answering Tricky Questions and Structuring Content

Change Management for Managers: The No Waffle Guide to Managing Change in the Workplace

How to Manage People: The No Waffle Guide to Managing Performance, Change and Stress in the Workplace

How to Manage Stress in the Workplace: The No Waffle Guide for Managers (EBook Only)

Manager's Guide to Providing Feedback: The No Waffle Guide to Providing Feedback and Rewards (EBook Only)

Coaching Skills for Managers: The No Waffle Guide to Getting the Best from Your Team (EBook Only)

The Counselling Sessions: Overcoming Feelings of Irritability and Anger in Relationships

The Counselling Sessions: Overcoming Low Mood and Depression

The Counselling Sessions: Overcoming Anxiety and Panic Attacks

www.ingramcontent.com/pod-product-compliance
Lightning Source LLC
Chambersburg PA
CBHW070935180526
45168CB00003B/1087